Cheetahs

by Darlene R. Stille

Science Adviser: Terrence E. Young Jr., M.Ed., M.L.S.,
Jefferson Parish (La.) Public Schools

Content Adviser: Jan Jenner, Ph.D.

Reading Adviser: Dr. Linda D. Labbo,
Department of Reading Education, College of Education,
The University of Georgia

COMPASS POINT BOOKS
MINNEAPOLIS, MINNESOTA

FIRST REPORTS

Compass Point Books
3109 West 50th Street, #115
Minneapolis, MN 55410

Visit Compass Point Books on the Internet at *www.compasspointbooks.com*
or e-mail your request to *custserv@compasspointbooks.com*

On the cover: Cheetah in a tree, Botswana

Photographs ©: Index Stock Imagery, cover, 19; DigitalVision, 4, 14, 26–27; Digital Stock, 5, 10–11;
PhotoDisc, 6, 33; Alain Pons/PhotoAlto, 7, 12, 20–21, 32; Creatas, 8, 16–17, 28, 43; Courtesy of Skulls
Unlimited International Inc., 9; Albert Copley/Visuals Unlimited, 13; Mary Ann McDonald, 15; Joe
McDonald, 18, 24; Erwin and Peggy Bauer/Tom Stack & Associates, 22; Anup Shah/Dembinsky Photo
Associates, 23; Mark J. Thomas/Dembinsky Photo Associates, 25; Bettmann/Corbis, 29; Mark N.
Boulton/Bruce Coleman Inc., 30–31; Victoria & Albert Museum, London/Art Resource, N.Y., 35;
AFP/Corbis, 36; Tom Brakefield/Corbis, 37; John Shaw/Bruce Coleman Inc., 38; Martin Harvey/
Gallo Images/Corbis, 39; Kennan Ward/Corbis, 40; Jason Lauré, 41.

Editor: Patricia Stockland
Photo Researcher: Svetlana Zhurkina
Designer/Page Production: Bradfordesign, Inc./Jaime Martens
Cartographer: XNR Productions, Inc.

Library of Congress Cataloging-in-Publication Data
Stille, Darlene R.
   Cheetahs / by Darlene R. Stille.
     p. cm. — (First reports)
   Includes bibliographical references and index.
   ISBN 0-7565-0576-3
   1. Cheetah—Juvenile literature. [1. Cheetah. 2. Endangered species.] I. Title. II. Series.
   QL737.C23S748 2004
   599.75'9—dc22   2003014421

Table of Contents

*NOTE: In this book, words that are defined in the glossary are in **bold** the first time they appear in the text.*

A Very Fast Cat

▲ *The cheetah can run as fast as a car.*

What can go from 0 to 45 miles (72 kilometers) per hour in about two seconds? What can reach speeds up to 70 miles (113 km) per hour? Hint: It's not a sports car. If you answered, "A cheetah," you would be right.

The cheetah is a member of the cat family. It is a wild cat, and it is the fastest cat alive. In fact, it is the fastest animal on land.

A cheetah can go so far with one **stride** that it looks like it is flying through the air. Cheetahs cannot run fast for very long, though. A cheetah running at top speed can go about 300 yards (274 meters), as far as two and a half football fields. Then it runs out of breath.

▲ *Sometimes cheetahs look like they are flying when they run.*

The Cheetah's Body

▲ *Black streaks on a cheetah's face look like tears. All cheetahs have these markings.*

The cheetah is a sleek-looking cat with a long tail and a small head. It has a yellowish coat with black spots. Black streaks running down from each eye look almost like tears. The fur on its throat and belly is white.

Unlike lions, cheetahs cannot roar. They only make small sounds. Sometimes a cheetah will sound like a bird chirping. Cheetahs can also hiss. When a cheetah is happy, it will purr like a house cat. A cheetah is much bigger than a house cat, though. It is about the size of a large dog.

▲ *This cheetah might look tough, but it cannot roar.*

▲ A cheetah's long legs and long spine help it leap forward and run fast.

The cheetah's body is built for speed. It has long, thin legs that help it run fast. Its spine acts like a spring to help it leap forward. It has claws that act like spikes on running shoes to keep it from slipping. It also has a large heart and large blood vessels. These give its body the oxygen it needs to run fast.

The cheetah has keen eyesight. It can see clearly for long distances. The cheetah also has sharp teeth, but its teeth are small for a big, wild cat. Other wild cats, such as the lion, have much larger teeth. The cheetah's teeth are smaller because there is no room in the cheetah's skull for the roots of big teeth.

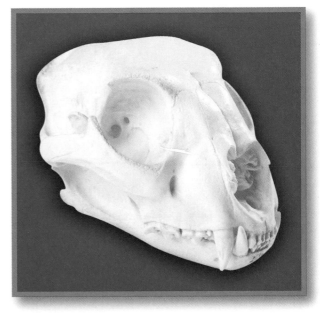

▲ *A cheetah's skull, showing the large nasal passages, large eye sockets, and sharp teeth*

▲ A cheetah's long, sleek body is built for speed.

Instead, the cheetah's skull has large nasal passages. These passages help carry air from the cheetah's nose to its lungs. The cheetah needs big nasal passages for breathing in lots of air while it runs. It also needs lots of air while it suffocates its **prey.** The cheetah does this by squeezing the prey's windpipe closed with its mouth.

Where Cheetahs Live

Cheetahs live mainly on grassy plains. Some live in areas with small trees and shrubs.

There may have been ancient cheetahs living in North America as long as 4 million years ago. Scientists found cheetah **fossils** in Texas, Nevada, and Wyoming.

▲ *The grassy plains of Africa are home to cheetahs.*

▲ *A cheetah fossil from North America, where they once roamed*

Cheetahs disappeared from North America long ago. Before 1900, hundreds of thousands of cheetahs lived all over Africa, in parts of Asia, and in India. Now, cheetahs live only in eastern, central, and southern Africa, especially in the countries of Namibia and South Africa. The country of Iran, in the Middle East, also has about 200 cheetahs.

Scientists say there may be as few as 5,000 cheetahs left or as many as 25,000. It is very difficult to count cheetahs in the wild because these animals are so shy. Many of them hide or run away before they can be counted. Scientists think that today the largest number of cheetahs live on the plains of Namibia. As many as 2,500 cheetahs may live there.

▲ *Savannah grass partially hides this cheetah.*

▲ *Cheetahs are very shy.*

How Cheetahs Live

▲ *Cheetahs use their speed for hunting food.*

Most cheetahs live alone. Females always live alone unless they are caring for young ones, called cubs.

Males sometimes live with their brothers. They never live with females or help raise cubs.

Cheetahs get their food by hunting. They hunt small to medium-size animals. They especially like African antelopes, including gazelles and impalas. Cheetahs hunt alone. They hunt early in the morning or late in the evening. A cheetah might climb a tree or a big termite mound to search with its keen eyes for prey.

▲ A cheetah in Samburu National Reserve, Kenya, looks for prey from atop a termite mound.

Imagine you could follow a cheetah when it goes hunting. It is early morning on the African plain when the cheetah spots a herd of gazelle. The cheetah silently stalks its prey. It creeps closer and closer to the herd through the tall grass and shrubs. It picks out a young gazelle on the edge of the herd.

▲ *Impalas, like these, and gazelle are often prey for cheetahs.*

Suddenly, the cheetah leaps out with a great burst of speed. The gazelle quickly turns and begins to run. The gazelle cannot outrun the cheetah. The cheetah grabs the gazelle by the throat and brings it to the ground. The cheetah then kills the gazelle by cutting off its air supply. The cheetah keeps its strong jaws clamped around the throat of the gazelle until it suffocates.

Cheetahs do not always catch their prey. Young cheetahs learning to hunt only catch about half of the animals they go after.

Cheetahs usually eat large prey on the spot where they killed it. First, the cheetah must

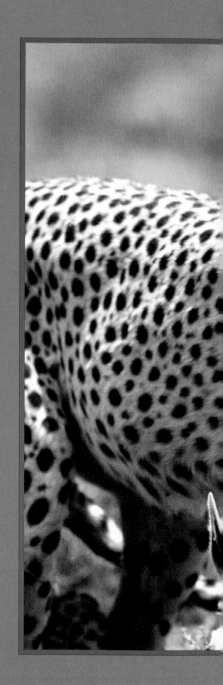

▲ A cheetah eats a gazelle on the spot where it was killed.

catch its breath. While the cheetah is resting, a lion or hyena might come along and try to steal the prey. Cheetahs do not have powerful bodies, so they cannot fight lions or hyenas. Cheetahs are not strong enough to drag the body of large prey to a hiding place. They must try to eat their prey before a bigger, stronger animal comes along.

▲ Cheetahs kill prey by cutting off its air supply.

Cheetah Cubs

▲ *A mother cheetah with her cubs*

Male and female cheetahs can mate at any time of the year to produce cubs. The mother cheetah gives birth to a litter, or group, of cubs about three months after she becomes pregnant. Her litter could be as

▲ *The gray fur on these cubs is called a mantle.*

small as one cub or as large as six cubs. Most litters average two to four cubs.

Cheetah cubs live in a dangerous world. Lions and other large animals kill many cheetah cubs. Cheetah cubs do have some protection. The cubs are covered with long, gray fur called a mantle. This mantle helps the cubs hide in the grass from lions and other natural enemies. The mother cheetah also moves her cubs from one hiding place to another every few days to help protect them. Still, 90 percent of cubs die in the wild.

Cheetah cubs follow their mother around and learn from her. At first, they eat prey that their mother has killed. Later, they learn from their mother how to hunt on their own.

▲ *Cubs learn to hunt by following their mother.*

▲ *Once a cheetah leaves its mother, it usually lives alone.*

Cheetah cubs stay with their mother for about 18 months. Then they go off to live by themselves. Cheetahs in the wild live about seven years. In zoos, they live about 12 years.

Endangered Cheetahs

▲ *Humans now use the land that once belonged to cheetahs.*

The cheetah is called an endangered animal because there are few cheetahs left in the world. There are three main reasons for this. The land that cheetahs and their prey once lived on has been made into farms, towns, and cities. There is no place left for the cheetahs to live. Also, hunters and poachers killed

▲ *Some of these fur coats from 1969 were made from cheetah skins.*

▲ *Some tourists in wildlife parks get close views of protected cheetahs.*

many cheetahs for their fur. In addition, some farmers feared these wild cats would kill their farm animals, so they, too, killed cheetahs.

Cheetahs are now protected in wildlife parks in Africa. However, lions and hyenas are also protected in these parks. Lions and hyenas take food from cheetahs. If they find a cheetah eating prey, the lions and hyenas will chase the cheetah away. The cheetah cannot fight back because the cheetah's thin, light body is made for running, not fighting.

▲ *Lions or hyenas could take away the prey this cheetah has caught.*

Lions and hyenas sometimes kill cheetah cubs. Where there are many lions and hyenas, there are very few cheetahs.

▲ *Lions like this one may kill cheetah cubs in nature parks.*

Cheetahs in Zoos

Long ago, kings and other rulers captured cheetahs. They put these graceful animals in their private zoos. They also tamed cheetahs. The rulers taught the tamed cheetahs to help them hunt other animals. The ancient Egyptians tamed cheetahs 5,000 years ago. A ruler in India 500 years ago captured 9,000 cheetahs and taught them to help him hunt deer.

Today, there are about 1,000 cheetahs in zoos around the world. There are about 300 cheetahs in zoos in the United States.

Cheetahs in traditional zoos almost never have cubs, and 30 percent of cubs that are born in **captivity** die. At first, scientists thought this was because all cheetahs are closely related. All cheetahs today are as closely related as identical twins.

However, scientists no longer think the shallow **gene pool** is the problem. Cheetahs have more

▲ This late 16th century watercolor shows Indian
Emperor Akbar the Great hunting with trained cheetahs.

▲ *These cubs were born in captivity at the Muenster Zoo in Germany.*

cubs if they live in zoos that are like the wild.
Cheetahs must not be kept in cages near other wild
cats that could frighten them. Males and females
must live in different areas, as they do in the wild.
Cheetahs also need running tracks where they can
exercise their sleek, fast bodies.

▲ *These cheetahs live in their natural environment on a wildlife reserve in South Africa.*

Protecting Cheetahs

▲ *Photographers on safari in Masai Mara National Reserve, Kenya, are able to take pictures of a cheetah.*

In order to protect cheetahs, scientists must learn more about them. Unfortunately, it is difficult to study this shy, fast-moving animal.

Scientists capture wild cheetahs. They put tags on the cheetahs. Then they can identify them if they capture them again. This can help scientists count cheetahs and learn things about the tagged cheetahs, such as whether they have cubs.

Sometimes they put radios on collars around the cheetahs' necks. The radios send signals that tell the scientists where the cheetahs are and how far they roam.

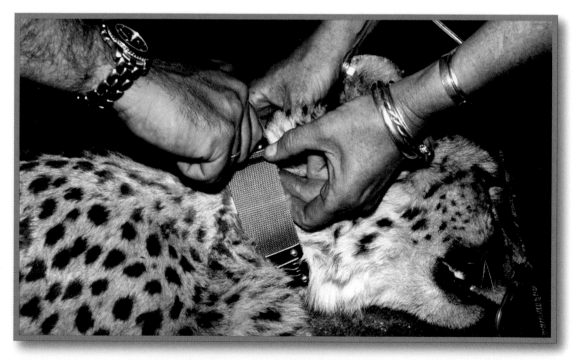

▲ *Scientists fit a cheetah with a radio collar.*

From this, scientists can learn how much land a cheetah needs to live on. Most cheetahs need 300 square miles (777 square kilometers) for their "home."

▲ *Tracking cheetahs in the wild helps scientists learn more about their habits, environments, and travel patterns.*

▲ *Animal catchers, including this man, rescue cheetahs from farmland, where they could be shot.*

Scientists are also looking for ways to protect cheetahs in Africa. Many cheetahs today live on farmland. Because farmers will kill the cheetahs to protect their farm animals, scientists have asked farmers to capture the cheetahs instead. They give farmers cages for catching cheetahs. The scientists then pick up the cheetahs and take them to a wild area.

Scientists also show farmers how to protect their herds from cheetahs. Large, fierce dogs can be put in with livestock herds. The dogs frighten the cheetahs away. Some farmers use donkeys to kick at cheetahs and drive them away.

Scientists also worry that disease may kill all the cheetahs. Because cheetahs are closely related, they could all get sick. One disease could kill all cheetahs because their bodies would not be able to fight off the germs. Because there are so few cheetahs left, everyone must work very hard to protect these beautiful wild cats.

▲ *Very few cheetahs are left in the wild.*

Glossary

captivity—being kept in a cage or locked up in some way

fossils—the remains of ancient life, such as bones and imprints of leaves

gene pool—the collection of genes of all the animals in an interbreeding group

prey—an animal that is hunted and eaten by other animals

stride—long steps; moving by taking long steps

Did You Know?

- Cheetahs don't need to drink water. Their prey provides the moisture they need.

- As cheetah cubs get older, they lose the long mane on their neck and shoulders.

- When chasing and catching prey, a cheetah's body temperature can reach 105 degrees Fahrenheit (41 degrees Celsius).

At a Glance

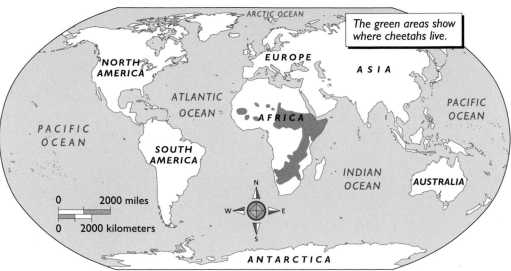

The green areas show where cheetahs live.

Range: Cheetahs live on the open plains and grasslands in parts of Africa and a small part of Iran.

Species: The cheetah species is called *Acinonyx jubatus.*

Size: Cheetahs are 2 to 3 feet (61 to 91 centimeters) tall at the shoulder and 3.5 to 4.5 feet (107 to 137 meters) long. They weigh between 86 to 143 pounds (39 to 64 kilograms). Males are generally bigger than females.

Diet: Cheetahs hunt small to medium-size animals, especially African antelopes, including gazelles and impalas.

Young: Most cheetahs have between two to four cubs, but litters can range from one to six.

Want to Know More?

At the Library

Cooper, Jason. *Cheetahs.* Vero Beach, Fla.: The Rourke Book Company, 2002.

Grimbly, Shona. *Cheetahs.* New York: Benchmark Books, 1999.

Kalz, Jill. *Cheetahs (Let's Investigate).* Mankato, Minn.: Creative Education, 2003.

Sullivan, Jody. *Cheetahs: Spotted Speedsters.* Mankato, Minn.: Bridgestone Books, 2003.

On the Web

For more information on cheetahs, use FactHound to track down Web sites related to this book.

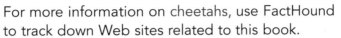

1. Go to *www.compasspointbooks.com/facthound*
2. Type in this book ID: 0756505763
3. Click on the *Fetch It* button.

Your trusty FactHound will fetch the best Web sites for you!

Through the Mail

Cheetah Conservation Fund
P.O. Box 1380
Ojai, CA 93024
805/640-0390
For information on cheetah conservation, research, and education

On the Road

San Diego Zoo
2920 Zoo Drive
San Diego, CA 92101
619/231-1515
To visit the Wild Animal Park and learn more about captive cheetah breeding

Index

About the Author

Darlene R. Stille is a science editor and writer. She has lived in Chicago, Illinois, all her life. When she was in high school, she fell in love with science. While attending the University of Illinois, she discovered that she also enjoyed writing. Today she feels fortunate to have a career that allows her to pursue both her interests. Darlene R. Stille has written more than 60 books for young people.